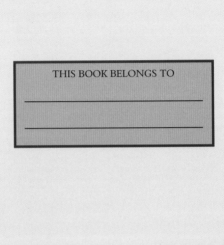

THIS BOOK BELONGS TO

_____

_____

REFLECTIONS
— ON —
SCOTLAND

I look upon Switzerland as an inferior sort of Scotland.
SYDNEY SMITH

In Scotland, the mountains are looked
on as eternal bodies.
JOHN MUIR

They've found buried treasure in Cladar Glen,
Fine gold coins of Dutch and Rhenish make,
Hard earned by a Highland soldier's wounds, then
Buried for his children's sake.
He died from some far off bayonet thrust,
Ne'er claimed his coins from the green glen's loam
Nor kept the promise writ in bitter dust:
"One glad day, I shall come home."
JAMES LENT

Glencoe, as full of history as any place in Scotland.

The impression Edinburgh has made on us is very great. It is quite beautiful, totally unlike anything else I have seen; and what is even more, Albert, who has seen so much, says it is unlike anything he ever saw; it is so regular, everything built of massive stone, there is not a brick to be seen anywhere.

QUEEN VICTORIA

The Royal Palace of Holyroodhouse, at the southern end of Edinburgh's Royal Mile.

Breathes there the man with soul so dead
Who never to himself hath said,
This is my own my native land!
Whose heart hath ne'er within him burned,
As home his footsteps he hath turned
From wandering on a foreign strand!

SIR WALTER SCOTT

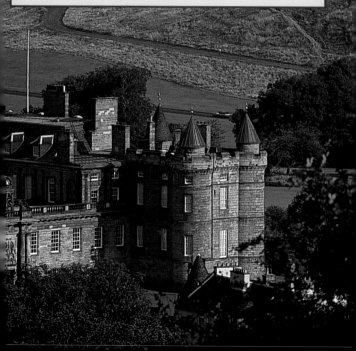

Gross upheavals of land that shaped Scotland down
the millennia and gave the country its
marvellous diversity have in different places
shaped the people too.
ROBERT PRENTICE

*The Stacks of Duncansby
off the Highland coast.*

Farewell to the Highlands, farewell to the North,
The birthplace of valour, the country of worth.
Wherever I wander, wherever I rove,
The hills of the Highlands for ever I love.
ROBERT BURNS

When the wind's in the north,
Hail comes forth;
When the wind's in the wast,
Look for a wat blast;
When the wind's in the soud,
The weather will be fresh and good;
When the wind's in the east,
Cauld and snaw comes neist.
TRADITIONAL

Yet, Caledonia, beloved are thy mountains,
Round their white summits though elements war.
LORD BYRON

*The winter snows begin to melt
in the Cairngorms.*

The people (quite a small crowd) threw bunches of heather as we passed. Heather is everywhere the decoration, and there is indeed no lovelier, prettier ornament.

QUEEN VICTORIA

Queen Victoria's beloved Balmoral.

In the Highlands, in the country places
Where the old plain men have rosy faces,
And the young fair maidens
Quiet eyes.
ROBERT LOUIS STEVENSON

Every year my heart becomes more fixed
in this dear paradise…
QUEEN VICTORIA

My heart's in the Highlands, my heart is not here;
My heart's in the Highlands, a'chasing the deer.
ROBERT BURNS

Tri aois duine aois feidh.
The stag that leads the herd hath thrice the age of any man.
OLD GAELIC PROVERB

*The sun sets over Loch Morlich,
near Aviemore.*

A native of Scotland considers himself a Scot before
he thinks of himself as a human being.
ANON

I am credibly informed that there is a Piper
in a neighbouring town that can only play one tune;
and was you to walk through every corner of that town,
you would hear that tune, and no other, in
the mouth of every child and servant there.
ROBERT BREMNER

They called on all to gather
From every scrog and scaur,
That loved their father's tartan
And the ancient game of war.
And down the watery valley
And up the windy hill,
Once more, as in the olden,
The pipes were sounding shrill.
ROBERT LOUIS STEVENSON

A piper at the Highland Games at Drumnadrochit,
on the banks of Loch Ness.

Speed bonnie boat like a bird on the wing,
'Onward' the sailors cry.
Carry the lad that's born to be king
Over the sea to Skye.
ROBERT LOUIS STEVENSON

A scene so rude, so wild as this,
Yet so sublime in barrenness...
SIR WALTER SCOTT

A summer's day high on the hills in Skye.

This castle hath a pleasant seat; the air
Nimbly and sweetly recommends itself
Unto our gentle senses.
WILLIAM SHAKESPEARE

*The great Baronial palace of Dunrobin Castle,
home of the Earls and Dukes of Sutherland.*

I love you for lulling me back into dreams
Of the blue Highland mountains and echoing streams.
THOMAS CAMPBELL

Where the pools are bright and deep,
Where the grey trout lies asleep…
JAMES HOGG

This is my country
The land that begat me,
These windy spaces
Are surely my own.
And those who here toil
In the sweat of their faces
Are flesh of my flesh,
And bone of my bone.
ALEXANDER GRAY

Summer twilight on the Island of Mull.

'Nothing but heather!' –
How marvellously descriptive!
And incomplete!
HUGH McDIARMUID

Over the heather the wet wind blows.
W.H.AUDEN

Here the splendid scenery begins – high, rugged and green hills… very fine large trees and beautiful pink heather, interspersed with bracken, rocks and underwood, in the most lovely profusion.

QUEEN VICTORIA

Early Summer in the Highlands.

Is a man who needs a pillow for his head a'nicht,
Fit to be a chieftain of the hills?
THE WARRIORS OF TORRIDON

*Eilean Donan Castle, overlooking the tranquil
waters of Loch Duich.*

Solitude, the romance and wild loveliness of
everything here, the absence of hotels and beggars,
the independent simple people, who all speak Gaelic here,
all make beloved Scotland the proudest,
finest country in the world.
QUEEN VICTORIA

Scotland shall have no need of castle walls
so long as it has its native thistles.
CELTIC CHIEFTAIN

$L$and of brown heath and shaggy wood,
Land of the mountain and the flood,
Land of my sires! what mortal hand
Can e'er untie the filial band,
That knits me to thy rugged strand!
SIR WALTER SCOTT

Perhaps it was our history of divided clans
making constant and careful society with one
another that made the Scots the finest builders
of bridges in the world.

J.R. M'CULLOCH

O Scotia! my dear, my native soil!
For whom my warmest wish to Heaven is sent!
Long may thy hardy sons of rustic toil
Be blest with health, and peace, and sweet content!
ROBERT BURNS

The Forth Railway Bridge, at night.

The Hebrides were set in a stormy sea at Creation,
so that no city should ever cross the sea to spoil them.
PETER McLAREN

As blooming Spring unbends the brow
of surly, savage Winter.
ROBERT BURNS

The scraggiest bit of heath in Scotland is more
to me than all the forest of Brazil.
THOMAS CARLYLE

First, in green apparel dancing,
The young Spring smiled with angel grace…
THOMAS CAMPBELL

What landscapes I read in the primrose's looks,
And what pictures of pebbled and minnowy brooks,
In the vetches that tangled their shore.
THOMAS CAMPBELL

*Puffins sunning themselves
on the cliffs of Staffa.*

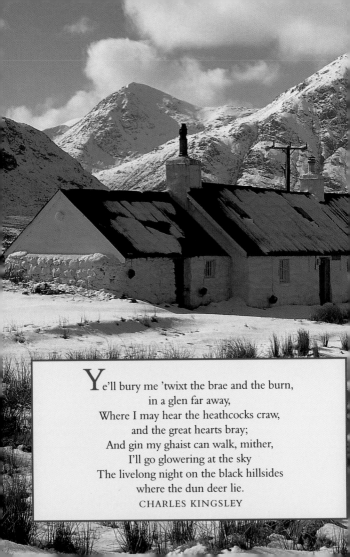

Ye'll bury me 'twixt the brae and the burn,
  in a glen far away,
Where I may hear the heathcocks craw,
  and the great hearts bray;
And gin my ghaist can walk, mither,
  I'll go glowering at the sky
The livelong night on the black hillsides
  where the dun deer lie.
CHARLES KINGSLEY

We took a most beautiful drive… through
mountain scenery – and with little huts, so low,
so full of peat smoke, that one could hardly see
anything for smoke.
QUEEN VICTORIA

*Black Rock Cottage, and the remote
beauty of Glen Etive.*

Every isle differs from the other in their fancy of making plaids, as to the stripes in breadth and colour. This humour is as different through the mainland of the Highlands insofar that they who have seen these places are able at the first view of a man's plaid to guess the place of his residence.

MARTIN MARTIN

INTER NOS II
BERISAY

And as long as I live, and where'er I may be,
I'll always remember my town by the sea.
ROBERT LOUIS STEVENSON

*Little fishing boats safely at anchor
in an island port.*

Such was the love of the Lady Devorgilla for her husband,
John Balliol, that when he died in 1269 she declared:
"I held his heart in life and I will hold it still now
that he is gone away." John's heart she had embalmed
and enwrapped in a costly casket of ivory, bound against
the ravages of the world with straps of silver.
For the 21 years that she lived on this earth without him,
my lady would daily address this casket, calling it

"My sweet, silent companion." At last came the day when the two hearts lay forever together. My lady had returned to her John, leaving behind a gift more precious than either ivory or silver – a new and lovely word in our language: the word 'sweetheart'.

ARTHUR TELLER

The ruins of Sweetheart Abbey, founded by Lady Devorgilla.

The hills covered with snow, the golden birch-trees
on the lower brown hills, and the bright afternoon
sky, were indescribably beautiful.
QUEEN VICTORIA

Oh my heart is fain to hear the soft wind blowing
Soughing through the fir-tops up on northern fells!
Oh, my eye's an ache to see the brown burns flowing
Through the peaty soil and tinkling heatherbells.
ADE SMITH

If it should happen to have been wet in the month
you chose, the water lilies in the lochs will make
you glad that you did take your holiday then.
COMPTON MACKENZIE

*Rhododendrons in flower
by the banks of Loch Clair, in Wester Ross.*

This profusion of eccentricities, this dream in masonry
and living rock is not a drop-scene in a theatre,
but a city in the world of everyday reality.
ROBERT LOUIS STEVENSON

Tenui musam meditamur avena –
'We cultivate literature upon a little oatmeal.'
MOTTO OF THE 19TH CENTURY
EDINBURGH REVIEW

If a body could just find oot the exac' proper proportion
and quantity that ought to be drunk every day, and keep
to that, I verily trow that he might leeve for ever,
without dying at a', and that doctors and kirkyards
would go oot o' fashion.
JAMES HOGG

*Edinburgh Castle, seen from Calton Hill
on a fine summer's morning.*

Ｆrom scenes like these old Scotia's grandeur springs,
That makes her loved at home, revered abroad,
Princes and lords are but the breath of kings,
An honest man's the noblest work of God.
ROBERT BURNS

---

*The massively strong artillery fortress,
Blackness Castle, a few miles from Edinburgh.*

The people of the coast are of domestic
and civilised habit, trusty, patient and urbane…
The Highlanders and people of the islands,
on the other hand, are a savage and untamed
nation, rude and independent.

JOHN OF FORDUN

ALSO IN THIS SERIES

Reflections on England

First published in Great Britain in 1998 by
JARROLD PUBLISHING LTD
Whitefriars, Norwich NR3 1TR

Developed and produced by
FOUR SEASONS PUBLISHING LTD
London, England

Text research by *Tom King*
Designed and typeset by *Judith Pedersen*
Printed in Dubai

ISBN 0 7117 0987 4

ACKNOWLEDGEMENTS

Four Seasons Publishing Ltd would like to thank all those
who kindly gave permission to reproduce the words and visual
material in this book; copyright holders have been identified where
possible and we apologise for any inadvertent omissions.

Front Cover: *Eilean Donan Castle* ERIC WEST
Cover Background: *Heather* Copyright © BOB GIBBONS/
ARDEA LONDON LTD
Back Cover: *Piper* DENNIS AVON
Title Page: *The Glenfinan monument* NEIL JINKERSON
Endpapers: *Kyle of Tongue* NEIL JINKERSON

Other photographs by: DENNIS AVON, J.A. BROOKS, G.A. DEY,
GORDON HENDERSON, NEIL JINKERSON, CHARLES J. NICHOLAS,
T. PARKER, ANDREW PERKINS, ERIC WEST.

All photographs copyright of *Jarrold Publishing Ltd.*
unless otherwise indicated.